I0815373

JUNK FOOD FOR THOUGHT

FAST FOOD FAST FACTS

KENNY ABDO

Fly!
An Imprint of Abdo Zoom
abdobooks.com

abdobooks.com

Published by Abdo Zoom, a division of ABDO, P.O. Box 398166, Minneapolis, Minnesota 55439. Copyright © 2026 by Abdo Consulting Group, Inc. International copyrights reserved in all countries. No part of this book may be reproduced in any form without written permission from the publisher. Fly!™ is a trademark and logo of Abdo Zoom.

Printed in the United States of America, North Mankato, Minnesota.
052025
092025

Photo Credits: Alamy, Bridgeman Images, Getty Images, Shutterstock
Production Contributors: Kenny Abdo, Jennie Forsberg, Grace Hansen
Design Contributors: Candice Keimig, Neil Klinepier, Laura Graphenteen

Library of Congress Control Number: 2024947738

Publisher's Cataloging-in-Publication Data

Names: Abdo, Kenny, author.
Title: Fast food fast facts / by Kenny Abdo
Description: Minneapolis, Minnesota : Abdo Zoom, 2026 | Series: Junk food for thought | Includes online resources and index.
Identifiers: ISBN 9781098288778 (lib. bdg.) | ISBN 9781098289478 (ebook) | ISBN 9781098289829 (Read-to-me ebook)
Subjects: LCSH: Junk food--Juvenile literature. | Food technology--Juvenile literature. | Food additives--Juvenile literature. | Fast foods--Juvenile literature. | Processed foods--Juvenile literature.
Classification: DDC 641.3--dc23

TABLE OF CONTENTS

FAST FOOD

From the markets of **Ancient Rome** to modern robot cooks, the history of fast food can be a real whopper!

THE EARLY JUNK

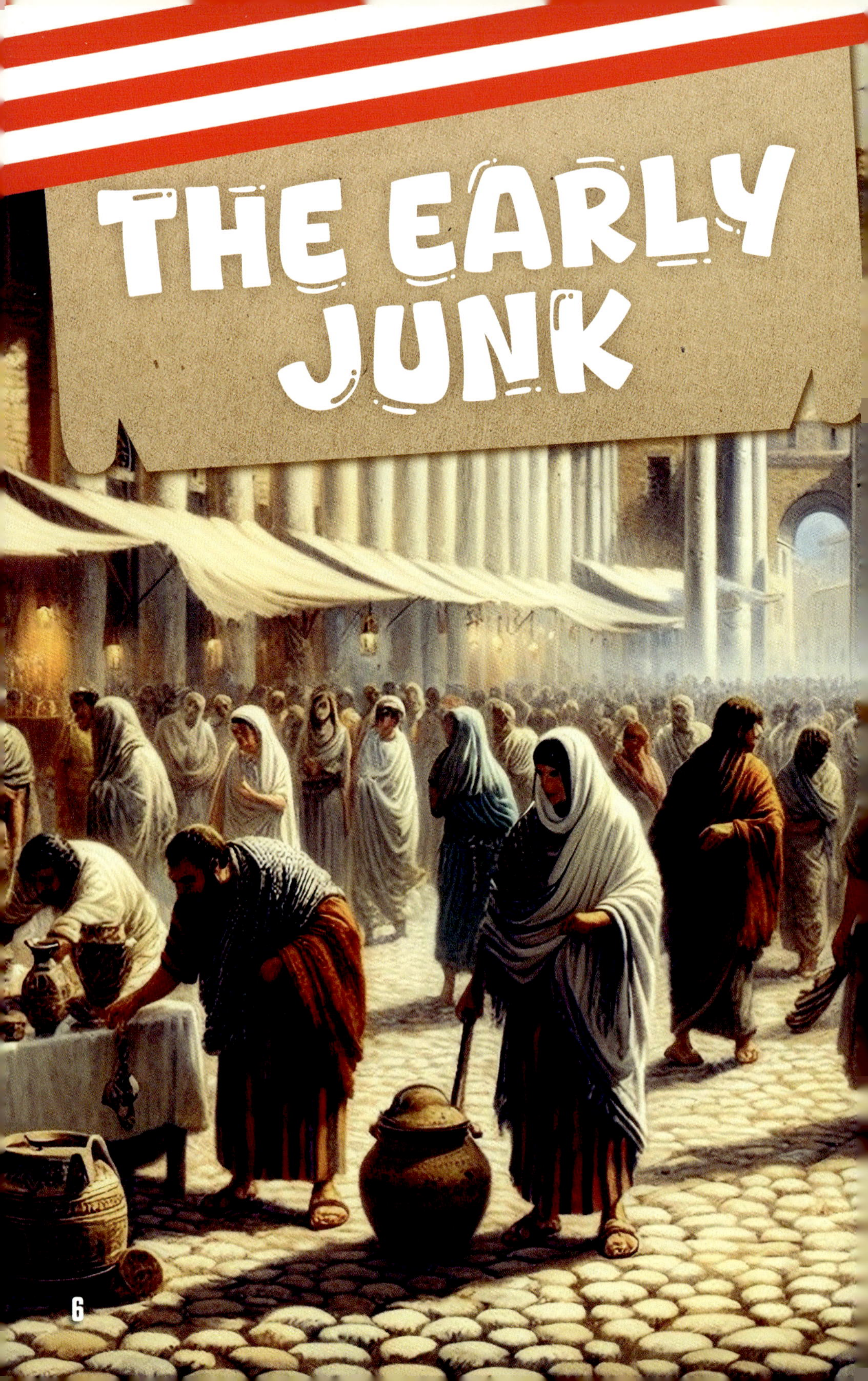

In **Ancient Rome**, people visited marketplaces to grab a bite to eat. Small stands sold ready-to-eat food such as soups and stews. It was almost like an ancient drive-through!

In the **Middle Ages**, lively fairs brought people together. They enjoyed fun, shopping, and dining! Vendors sold hot pies, pretzels, and nuts. With entertainment and fast food, people could spend all *knight* there!

THE FOOD PROCESS JUNK

Cities grew very quickly throughout the **Industrial Revolution**. Busy workers needed quick meals that matched the pace of the new cities. Street vendors made it easy to grab a bite on the go. This marked the start of fast food for fast lifestyles!

'HERE WE A
STOP HERE!
THIS IS THE ONLY ORIGINAL Nathan's FAMOUS
ORIGINAL
NATHANS
FAMOUS
FRANKFURTERS
from a HOT
to a national
OPEN ALL Y
ALL OUR FOOD FRESH
FRANKFURTER
HAMBURGER
ROAST BEEF
Nathan's
ROOT BEER 5¢
CHOW MEIN BARBECUE
BEER ON DRAUGHT
ORANGE PINEAPPLE GRAPE 5¢
FRANKFURTER
HAMBURGER ROAST BEEF
FRANKFURTERS
OPEN ALL YEAR
HOT FRANKFURTER ON TOASTED ROLL
FRAN
GRAPE
PINEAPPL
No Extr

In 1916, Nathan Handwerker opened a hot dog stand at Coney Island. The delicious franks were an instant hit. Today, Nathan's has more than 300 locations worldwide. The yearly July 4th hot dog eating contest continues to celebrate the fast food icon and gross out fans!

Whispers of a tiny, square hamburger spread in Kansas in 1921. The fast service also stirred up curiosity. Known as the first hamburger **chain**, White Castle continues to serve its famous sliders today in over 350 locations throughout the United States!

In 1948, married couple Harry and Esther Snyder married two ideas together: a simple menu and fresh ingredients. From there, a loyal fan base grew.

People also loved that the food was delivered to their cars. Today, In-N-Out continues to be a favorite among burger lovers!

Back in 1955, brothers Richard and Maurice McDonald shook up the fast-food scene. Their restaurant used the Speedee Service System to dish out burgers quickly.

McDonald's is now one of the largest fast food **chains** in the world. You can find its golden arches in more than 100 countries!

COMMONWEALTH OF KENTUCKY
BIRTHPLACE OF
KENTUCKY FRIED CHIC
COURT & CAFE
ENTUCKY
Corbin, Ky
5 Miles North

Colonel Harland Sanders started serving fried chicken at his gas station in 1952. The Kentuckian made it special by using his recipe of 11 herbs and spices. The chicken was an instant, crispy hit. Today, KFC salutes from 150 countries!

Taco Bell first rang in 1962. The tasty Tex-Mex food got the ball rolling for **fast-casual** dining to grow. Chipotle came onto the scene in the late '90s. They focused on fresh ingredients and tailored meals. Able to choose their favorite ingredients to create burritos and bowls, fans had a lot to taco 'bout!

CaliExpress **debuted** in 2023. It is leading the way in **automated** fast food service. These robot restaurants can quickly cook and serve meals. Other popular **chains**, like McDonald's, are also starting to use this technology. It is a race to the future!

THE TUMMY ACHE

Today, fast food **chains** are focusing more on the environment. In 2019, Burger King launched the Impossible Whopper. It helped promote plant-based options for those who want the fast food lifestyle without eating meat. McDonald's planned to move toward all **sustainable** packaging by 2025.

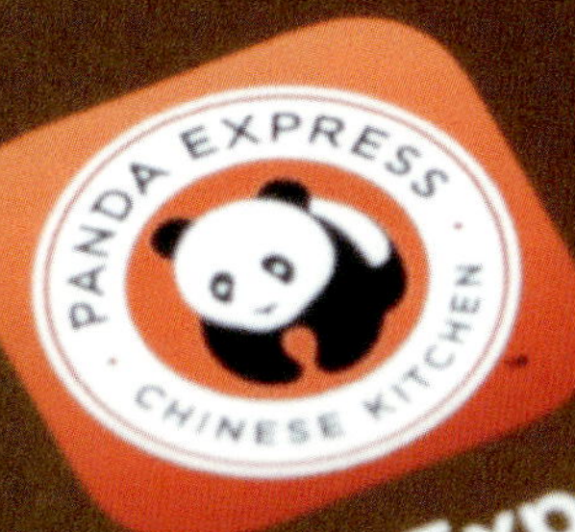

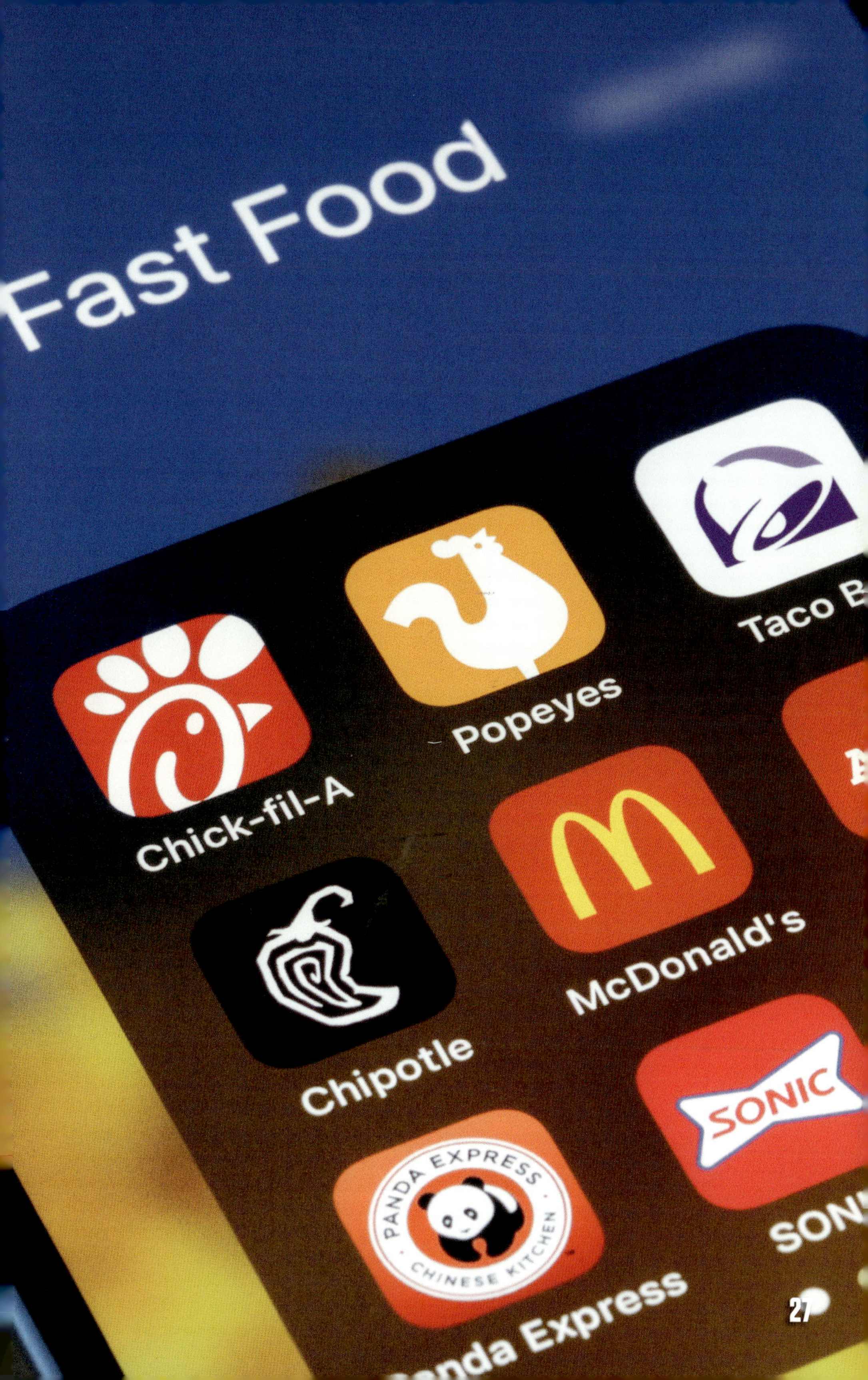
Fast Food
Chick-fil-A
Popeyes
Taco B
McDonald's
Chipotle
SONIC
PANDA EXPRESS
CHINESE KITCHEN
anda Express

The quick and savory history of fast food has left a lasting impact on our culture. Its legacy will stand the test of time with no expiration date!

GLOSSARY

Ancient Rome – (753 BCE–476 CE) A small civilization that grew into an empire that developed laws, government, and culture.

automated – tasks that are performed by machines or computers without needing human control.

chain – restaurants that serve food quickly and efficiently, with many locations found around the world.

debut – a first appearance.

fast-casual – a restaurant that serves quick, high-quality ingredient meals with little to no table service.

Industrial Revolution – starting in the mid-18th century, a period marked by major changes in how products were made.

Middle Ages – (500–1500 CE) A period in Europe that is known for the spread of Christianity and the growth of kingdoms.

sustainable – of or related to a method of managing or using a resource so that the resource is never used up.

JUNK FOOD FOR THOUGHT

ONLINE RESOURCES

To learn more about fast food, please visit abdobooklinks.com or scan this QR code. These links are routinely monitored and updated to provide the most current information available.

INDEX